# *Lucky to be Alive:*
## *Stories of Survival*

Evelina Zarkh, Ellen Goodenow,
and Christopher Mitten

## SCHOLASTIC INC.

New York   Toronto   London   Auckland   Sydney
Mexico City   New Delhi   Hong Kong

**Cover illustration and interior illustrations
by Jacques Lamontagne**

6   7   8   9   10        23        10 09

# Contents

# Introduction

Have you ever been lost? Have you ever been afraid of some noise at night that you couldn't name? Most of us have been lost or afraid at one time or another, even if it was just for a short while.

But imagine being lost in the jungle, stranded in the middle of the ocean, or trapped in the fiery mouth of a volcano. You're hurt. No help arrives. You're surrounded by danger. Night falls. You are scared. And you are alone. It's like a nightmare—only you're awake.

In this book, you will meet ordinary people who survived hungry animals, deadly fumes, and raging seas. You will learn how they kept up hope even when all hope had gone.

Here are three stories about people who cheated death. And their stories go to show that sometimes the will to live is the strongest force in nature.

# 1 The Mouth of the Volcano

Hollywood movies are famous for special effects. But some effects can't be faked. So when one movie called for a volcano scene, producers decided to film the real thing. They sent a helicopter crew to shoot Hawaii's Kilauea, the world's most active volcano.

At the time of filming, Kilauea had been erupting steadily for ten years. Every day it pumped huge clouds of poisonous smoke into the air. It produced a steady river of red-hot lava six miles long. And inside one of its large craters was a **smoldering** lava pit nearly 120 feet deep. Filming this volcano was extremely dangerous. But the film crew was one of the best in the business.

The crew consisted of two camera experts, Michael Benson and Chris Duddy, and an ace pilot named Craig Hosking. Each had extensive experience doing dangerous film shoots. Unfortunately, this journey into the mouth of an active volcano would turn out to be their ultimate test.

To shoot the footage that was needed, they had to go down into the **murky** smog of the volcano's large crater. It was hard to see, and flying conditions were dangerous. At first, the job went smoothly. But after a few minutes, disaster struck. The blades of the helicopter hit a wall that was hidden by smoke. The crew had no time to react. The helicopter crashed inside the volcano.

Amazingly, none of the crew members were injured. But they did have one enormous problem. They were 150 feet deep inside the crater of a volcano. Next to them was a deadly pool of lava. Poisonous gases swirled around them. They wouldn't be able to survive for long down there. And who would be able to get them out?

The group took a few minutes to think about their situation. Michael and Chris decided to climb up the volcano's rim. Craig chose to stay with the helicopter. He thought he could get the radio working so that he could call for help.

The volcano's smoke was very thick. After a few seconds of climbing, Chris and Michael could no longer see the bottom of the crater. As they slowly climbed up the sheer wall, they both got stuck on ledges far above the crater floor. They couldn't climb any higher. They couldn't climb back down. They were trapped. And the fumes inside the volcano were so thick that they could no longer see one another. Each was alone.

Finally, Craig got the radio working and called for help. After two hours rescue helicopters arrived. The problem was that the smoke was so thick that rescuers couldn't see Chris and Michael. And when the rescue team got a general idea of where Michael and Chris were, they couldn't get close enough to the crater wall to perform a rescue. Only Craig could be lifted out of the crater. But it was so cloudy that Michael and Chris didn't even know that their friend had been saved. When Craig stopped replying to their calls, they thought he had died.

After a while the noise from the rescue helicopters faded. Michael and Chris realized that help wasn't coming, so they prepared to spend the night.

Soon harsh winds began to blow. Rain pelted the two survivors. As daylight faded, it also became extremely cold. But there was nothing the men could do. They had to wait for dawn for rescue attempts to begin again. Their only comfort was the sound of a whistle that the rescue crew blew every hour. The sound let Michael and Chris know that they had not been forgotten.

By the next morning, the situation had grown worse. The volcanic fumes were still swirling around the men, but now the storms were getting stronger. This made it even harder for the rescue crews to reach them. Eventually Chris lost patience. The ledge he was on was about thirty feet higher than

Michael's. He decided to attempt the **vertical** climb to the top. He thought that he'd rather die trying to escape than die clinging to that ledge. With a burst of energy, Chris propelled himself up the rim. It took him an hour to climb about forty feet. But eventually he made it. Now only Michael was left.

Michael continued to cling to his ledge. A large cinder fell into the lava as Chris climbed out. Michael couldn't see because of the smoke, but he could hear it fall. He thought it was his friend, Chris, falling to his death. So, Michael decided to stay where he was. It began to seem like he would never escape. Still, he gripped his ledge. He braved the harsh weather, and did whatever he could to avoid the toxic fumes. But he was growing sicker and sicker. The day passed. Still no rescue squad had shown up to save him. Michael would have to spend another sleepless and terrifying night on the ledge.

Finally, the next morning, help arrived. The weather improved and a helicopter got as close as it could to the crater. They had to be very careful, or they would have the same kind of accident that the film crew had. But the rescuers had a plan. From the helicopter, they dangled a 70-foot long line near Michael. It had a large basket attached to it. They wanted to use it to lift Michael out of the volcano.

Michael was cold and tired. And he was sick from the toxic fumes. It wouldn't be easy for him to get hold of the basket and line. Plus, **visibility** was still poor. He could only see a few feet in front of him. But after four attempts, he was finally able to grab hold of the basket. Slowly the rescue team pulled him to safety high above the mouth of the volcano.

The three men didn't recover right away. Even though they escaped the volcano, they had still been made ill by the poisonous gases. Michael, who had been in the volcano the longest, had to be hospitalized. But he soon got better.

The fact that Michael, Chris, and Craig were able to escape from an active volcano proves they had extraordinary survival skills. But next time, they might not want to find out the hard way.

If you had been stuck inside the volcano, what would you have done?

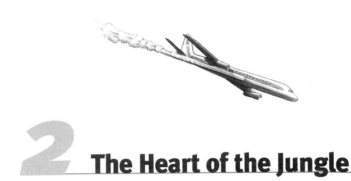

# 2 The Heart of the Jungle

The Amazon jungle in South America is wild and mysterious. Thousands of rare plants and animals live there. And only a small number of people do. Parts of it are still unexplored. Scientists are only beginning to understand this place. But one thing is for sure. The jungle contains many dangers.

No one understood the dangers better than Juliane Koepcke. Her parents had worked in the jungle for years. They were scientists who studied animals. Juliane had spent some time with them at their research station. But for the rest of the year, she went to school in Lima, Peru.

It was on a trip from Lima that the

unthinkable happened. It was Christmas Eve, 1971. Juliane Koepcke was seventeen years old. She and her mother got on a plane headed for the research station in the jungle. They planned to celebrate the holiday there with Juliane's father.

Juliane's mother was nervous as the plane took off. There had been trouble on this flight before. Then, 40 minutes after takeoff, the small plane started shaking. It had hit a pocket of rough air.

Soon the plane was in the middle of a terrible thunder and lightning storm. Juliane could see that they were very close to the mountains. Then the plane's wing caught on fire. Tragedy struck. Juliane felt herself flying through the air. Then she lost **consciousness**.

Hours later, Juliane woke up. She was still in her seat. Her seatbelt was on. But she wasn't in the plane anymore. She was in the jungle. Dazed, Juliane looked for her mother. But her mother was gone. The seats beside her were now empty.

Juliane was terrified. Her plane had crashed

in the middle of the Amazon. Her face was scratched. Her collarbone was broken. She had deep cuts on her body. Pieces of the plane were everywhere. Juliane could see other passengers from the plane. But none of them moved. She realized that she was alone. And she knew she had to find help fast. She was hurt. She wouldn't be able to survive in the jungle for long.

Juliane got out of her seat. She looked around for anything that would be useful. She found a cake and a bag of candy that had fallen from the plane. Then she started walking. She had been in the jungle many times, but never by herself.

She remembered that her parents had told her that if she ever got lost, she should find a river and follow it. Water would lead her to people. So Juliane looked for water. After a while she found a stream. She followed the stream. Eventually, the stream turned into a river.

Juliane knew that Indians build their towns near rivers. She needed to find a town. She knew her search would go quicker if she swam the river instead of walking next to it.

But rivers in the jungle are full of danger. In these rivers live fish called piranhas. Piranhas eat animal flesh. If piranhas smell blood in the water, they will attack the bleeding animal. In seconds, they can eat all the flesh from the bone. Juliane had many bleeding cuts. She also saw caiman by the river. Caiman are in the same family as crocodiles and alligators. They kill their prey by pulling them underwater and drowning them.

Juliane was scared, but the river was her only hope. She swam and swam. She didn't find any towns. But she did manage to stay alive.

After swimming for a long time, Juliane decided to walk for a while. But surviving on land wasn't much easier. As Juliane walked through the jungle, flies attacked her. They landed on her open cuts and began laying eggs in them. Soon she was covered with worms.

At night the jungle was even scarier. Many animals came out to hunt. Juliane was scared because she knew that one of these animals might try to attack her. And she couldn't sleep because everywhere she went, she heard insects and felt them crawling on her. The insects could be dangerous, too.

After many days of swimming and walking, Juliane was tired and in pain. She came across more pieces from her airplane wreck. She could hear rescue planes flying overhead. But they could not see her through the thick jungle canopy overhead. The jungle surrounded her and would not let her go.

But Juliane would not give up. She found another river. She made a raft out of logs and vines. She floated down the river on her raft. Suddenly she saw a canoe on the banks of the river. A sign of human life! Finally there was hope. She crawled out of the water.

Juliane wanted to rest there. She wanted someone to find her, but she didn't know if anyone would ever come back for the canoe. She thought about using it to travel further down the river. Maybe there was a town nearby.

But Juliane did not want to take something that didn't belong to her. She felt that stealing was wrong. So she decided to wait by the canoe and hope that its owner

would return. Juliane had spent nine days, all alone, in the heart of the jungle.

After a while, a woodcutter found Juliane by the canoe. He saw her little raft and her cuts and bruises. He saw that she was in trouble. He took her to a nearby town.

When Juliane got to the town, the people offered her food. She hadn't eaten anything but cake and candy in over a week! Still, she said that her stomach had shrunk and she wasn't hungry anymore. So the people helped her tend to her wounds. They helped her wash the bugs off her body.

Soon Juliane was taken to a hospital. There, she was reunited with her father. Slowly her wounds healed. She got her strength back. She returned to Germany, where her family was originally from. But Juliane's mother, who had been sitting right next to her on the plane, was never found. Of the 91 passengers on her plane, Juliane was the only one to survive. Everyone else on board, including the plane's crew, had died in the crash.

After several months, Juliane returned to

Peru to finish her studies. She took another plane. Reporters asked Juliane if she was afraid to fly. She told them that no, she wasn't afraid. Accidents can happen to anybody, she said.

Somehow, that thought is not exactly comforting—unless you're a real survivor like Juliane.

How can you tell that Juliane is a courageous person?

# 3 The Middle of the Ocean

Are you adventurous? Perhaps you would like to travel someday. You might even travel around the world. But would you travel by boat? And would you be willing to face the fiercest ocean in the world—alone?

This was Tony Bullimore's dream. He was an experienced sailor. He loved the sea and he had sailed alone many times. Then he entered a race that would give him the ride of his life.

On January 5, 1997, he set out from France. He was 56 years old. He would sail nonstop in his boat, the Exide Challenger, all the way around the world—solo.

Tony sailed south. He planned to take the shortest **route**. He wanted to win the race.

But the route was also very dangerous. It would take him where the waters of the Atlantic, Pacific, and Indian oceans meet. This area is known for huge storms and deadly seas.

Other sailors took similar routes. Tony knew that they were nearby. But as he sailed on, he left the other sailors behind. Soon Tony and his boat were all alone on the open sea between Australia and Antarctica.

For a while, it was clear sailing. But one day Tony saw dark clouds coming. He was heading into a storm. He did everything he could to prepare for it. Before long, the wind was blowing hard. And the boat was crashing against 60-foot waves.

Tony steered through the storm for eight hours, but he and his boat were taking a beating. Steering was hard work and he soon grew tired. He needed to take a break. So he decided to let the boat sail on autopilot. He went below deck to eat and rest.

That evening Tony heard a loud crack. His boat, the Exide Challenger, had turned upside-down, with Tony trapped in the cabin beneath!

The boat's keel, the fin-like board on the bottom of the boat, had broken off. With the keel gone, there was little chance of getting the boat to stand up straight again. He tried to remain calm.

Tony had some emergency signals with him. They would let race headquarters know where he was. Even though he wanted to **alert** people to his accident right away, he decided to use only one of the signals. He didn't want to use them all up right away in case he was stuck for a long time. He pushed the first signal out of the window. He hoped it would reach the water's surface. He wanted to let race headquarters know that he was in danger.

Tony also put on his waterproof survival suit. If not for the suit, he would have frozen in minutes. The suit was made of a special material. The material helped keep him warm and dry. Instead of going outside to sit on the boat's upturned bottom, he stayed underneath the boat. Water had seeped in, but there was still air trapped inside the cabin.

So Tony built a hammock on a small shelf above the water line. He crawled onto the hammock. He waited. And he thought about how to stay alive.

Tony tried to free a life raft that was attached to the boat. It was underwater. So he had to make many trips. But the water was very cold. He could hold his breath for only short periods of time. So he had to work in short bursts.

While trying to untie the raft, Tony had another accident. He cut off a part of his finger. He returned to his shelf, wounded and tired. He was frustrated. He would have to forget about freeing the life raft.

For four days he lay on his hammock. He was hurt. He was cold and wet. The only food he had was a little bit of chocolate. He had to make his drinking water with a hand pump. It took 1,000 pumps to make one cup of water.

Tony hoped that help was on the way, but he was not sure. He knew he would have to hang on for as long as possible just in case. Tony waited and waited. He slept and rested most of the time. He tried to save his energy. He tried to stay calm.

Meanwhile, the people at race headquarters had received Tony's signal. They called on the Royal Australian Navy to rescue him. But finding the Exide Challenger was not easy for the rescuers. They sent helicopters to look for his upside-down boat. They looked and looked. They even rescued another sailor whose boat had overturned. Tony was still missing.

The rescue team finally saw Tony's boat floating, bottom up, in the ocean. But they could not see Tony. They assumed that he was dead. They didn't think he'd survive in the middle of the freezing ocean. They thought that his lifeless body might be inside the boat. Still, there was a possibility that maybe, just maybe, Tony was still alive.

The rescue team dropped special **sensors** next to the boat to find out if Tony was inside. The sensors showed that there was someone in the boat. But the team still couldn't tell if Tony was alive or dead. So they decided to send a rescue ship, just in case.

Tony had heard the Navy helicopters flying overhead. He was anxious to get to safety. He thought about swimming out of the boat so the helicopters could see him. But he knew that the water was freezing cold. He would not be able to survive for very long in the water. What if the people in the helicopters did not see him in time? He might freeze to death! Tony decided to be patient. He would stay where he was and give the rescuers a chance to find him.

Back home, Tony's family and friends watched news of the accident on TV. They saw pictures of Tony's upturned boat floating helplessly in the water. Like the rescuers, they feared the worst. No one knew that Tony was still alive, trapped under his own boat.

The Australian Navy sent a rescue ship to get closer to the upturned boat. They still didn't know if Tony was alive. And the rescue ship was slowed by bad weather.

At last the rescue ship made it to the Exide Challenger. The rescuers sent out a raft. They banged on the boat. Tony banged back. The rescuers couldn't believe it! They prepared to get Tony out from under the Exide Challenger.

But Tony was so happy he couldn't wait any

longer. He swam out of the boat before the divers could get to him. And after four days lost at sea, Tony was rescued.

The rescue ship took Tony to New Zealand. Eventually, he went back home to England. Everywhere Tony went, people treated him like a hero. That's because it takes a lot of courage to stay calm and survive in a tough situation. Like all the other heroes in this book, Tony never gave up hope.

What do think was the hardest part of Tony's struggle?

# Glossary

**alert** to warn someone that there might be danger

**consciousness** the state of being awake and able to think and perceive

**murky** dark, cloudy, or gloomy

**route** the road or path used to get from one place to another

**sensors** instruments that can detect changes in heat, sound, pressure, etc.

**smoldering** burning and smoking slowly with no flames

**vertical** upright, or straight up and down

**visibility** ability to see